FOOTBALL SUPERSTARS

NEYMAR RULES

Hi, pleased to meet you.

We hope you enjoy our book about Neymar!

I'm **VARbot** with all the facts and stats!

WELBECK

SIMON

DAN

VAR

Published in 2022 by Welbeck Children's Limited
part of the Welbeck Publishing Group
Based in London and Sydney
www.welbeckpublishing.com
Text © 2021 Simon Mugford
Design & Illustration © 2021 Dan Green
ISBN: 978-1-78312-967-6

Writer: Simon Mugford
Designer and Illustrator: Dan Green
Design manager: Sam James
Executive editor: Suhel Ahmed
Production: Freencky Portas

A catalogue record for this book is available from the British Library.

Printed in the UK
10 9 8 7 6 5 4 3 2

Statistics and records correct as of November 2020

FOOTBALL SUPERSTARS

NEYMAR

RULES

SIMON MUGFORD　　　DAN GREEN

CONTENTS

NEYMAR!

NEYMAR!

Neymar is one of the

BEST FOOTBALLERS

IN THE WORLD!

Everyone knows that!

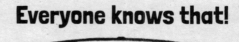
He's definitely the most expensive!

6

But what is it that makes Neymar such a **FANTASTIC, AMAZING** and **AWESOME PLAYER?**

THIS BOOK IS ALL ABOUT HIM — SO LET'S FIND OUT!

NEYMAR'S SUPER SKILLS

Speed
Quick on his feet – he easily gets past defenders.

Dribbling
One of the best at getting past defenders with the ball stuck to his feet.

Tricks
Performs mind-boggling back-heels, fancy flicks and super step-overs.

Touch
Able to deliver a killer pass or shoot as soon as he gets the ball.

Best of all, as a **SUPERSTAR** forward, Neymar scores **loads and loads** of **amazing**

GOALS!

NEYMAR IN NUMBERS

The numbers that show Neymar's **awesomeness:**

2 ... South American **Footballer of the Year** Awards

2 ... La Liga wins with **Barcelona**

1 ... Champions League win with **Barcelona**

3 ... Ligue 1 wins with **Paris Saint-Germain**

In **Brazil,** where Neymar is from, football

is known as

THE BEAUTIFUL GAME.

BRAZIL

BRASILIA

RIO DE JANEIRO

SÃO PAULO

Brazilian footballers are famous for their **stylish movement** and **cool skills.**

Brazil has produced some of the **best footballers ever** to play the game.

PELÉ

Won the **World Cup** three times. Maybe the **best player of all time.**

KAKA

Legendary playmaker at **Milan** and **Real Madrid.** Winner of the **World Cup, Champions League** and the **Ballon d'Or.**

NEYMAR I.D.

NAME: *Neymar da Silva Santos Júnior*

NICKNAME: *Joia (Gem), Juninho*

DATE OF BIRTH: *5 February 1992*

PLACE OF BIRTH: *Mogi das Cruzes, Brazil*

HEIGHT: *1.75 m*

POSITION: *Forward*

CLUBS: *Santos, Barcelona, Paris Saint-Germain*

NATIONAL TEAM: *Brazil*

LEFT OR RIGHT-FOOTED: *Right*

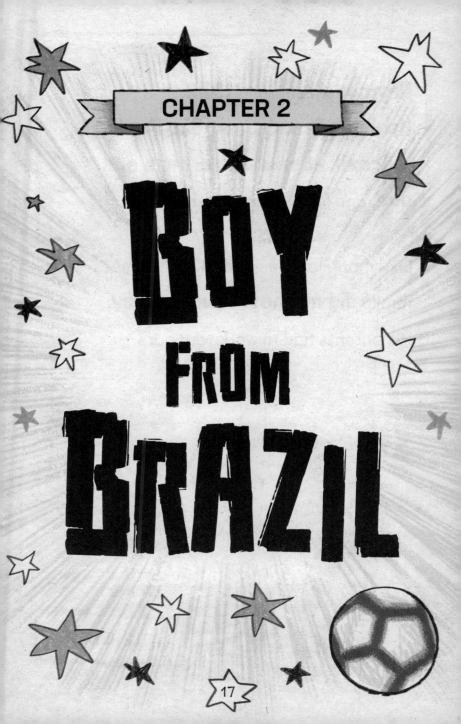

Neymar was born in **1992**, in **Mogi das Cruzes,** near **São Paulo** in **Brazil.** He lived with his **mum and dad,** and later, his younger **sister.**

Like many families in **Brazil,** Neymar's family **did not have much money.** His parents had to work very hard.

LITTLE NEYMAR

Neymar's dad had been a professional **footballer,** but he had to stop playing when he was hurt in a **car accident.**

Why is he called **Neymar Junior?**

Because his dad is called **Neymar,** too!

21

To **save money,** Neymar's family moved into his **grandparents' house** in **São Vicente.**

They didn't have **much space,** but Neymar would somehow run, jump, and kick a ball **all over the house.**

CRACK!

He even made his **little sister and cousins** join in, too!

IT DROVE HIS PARENTS **CRAZY!**

JÚNIOR!

One day in **1998, Neymar's dad** was playing in a **beach football match.** He took his son along to watch him play.

But **Neymar** could not sit still. He didn't have a ball, but he **ran, jumped** . . . and **danced,** up and down the stands.

RUN

JUMP

DANCE

A **football coach** called **Betinho** spotted him.

WOW, THIS KID CAN REALLY MOVE!

And that's how it started.

Betinho became Neymar's coach.

"OF ALL THE BOYS I DEALT WITH, NONE OF THEM HAD WHAT NEYMAR HAS."

Betinho

CHAPTER 3

StREETS AnD BEACHES

Futsal is a version of football played on a **small, hard court**, with a **smaller ball**. It is very popular in **Brazil.** Futsal players move **very quickly and skilfully** and learn lots of **cool tricks.**

NICE MOVE, **NEYMAR!**

With Betinho **as his coach,** Neymar quickly became a star on the futsal courts.

When he was old enough to go out and play on his own, **Neymar** would play **street football** as often as he could. He was the **best player by far** and people would gather to watch.

WOW, WHAT A PLAYER!

Neymar loved **entertaining the crowd** with his **tricks and skills.**

HE WAS BORN TO BE A SUPERSTAR!

By the time Neymar was 11, his family were **living by the sea** in **Santos,** a small town not far from **São Paulo.** Beach football was **THE** game to play there.

Playing **barefoot on the sand**, Neymar learned awesome **balance** and **control**.

What do you do when you score a goal in beach football?

SHELL-A-BRATE!

Groan!

33

Neymar started playing futsal for **Gremetal**, where **Betinho was a coach.** Nobody could beat Gremetal when Neymar played!

He also played football for the youth team in local side **Portuguesa Santista.**

The cool young kid with amazing skill was becoming a **local legend** in Santos!

THWACK!

THAT KID IS REALLY GOOD!

YUP!

Zito was a **legend in a Brazilian football.**

In 2003, he was a scout for **Santos.** He saw

Neymar play and said:

"I'VE NEVER SEEN ANYONE LIKE THIS KID. WE NEED TO SIGN HIM!"

Zito

CHAPTER 4

THE FAME GAME

Neymar is more than one of the **world's best-known footballers** - he is one of the most **famous people on the planet!**

With around **250 MILLION** followers on Facebook, Instagram and Twitter, he is the world's **second most** popular athlete on **social media.**

HE HASN'T GOT AS MANY FOLLOWERS AS **ME!**

Ronaldo

According to *Forbes Magazine*, he was the world's **fourth-highest paid athlete** in **2020**.

1 **ROGER FEDERER** $106.3 MILLION

2 **CRISTIANO RONALDO** $105 MILLION

3 **LIONEL MESSI** $104 MILLION

4 **NEYMAR** $95.5 MILLION

Neymar's **famous face** has appeared

on the cover of *TIME* magazine . . .

And in adverts for . . .

Energy drinks . . .

Trainers . . .

and video games!

41

Neymar loves a **good birthday party** -
especially his own! His fancy parties are
huge events, and he invites lots of his
celebrity friends and **famous players**.

Justin Bieber

Lewis Hamilton

Kylian Mbappé

43

Neymar is a big fan of changing his hairstyles. **Which one is your favourite?**

SPIKY

SHORT

SLICK

FLUFFY

DAN'S CUTZ

MOHAWK

MOHAWK TAIL

Fancy a trim?

THE TRUMP

THE LIONEL (MESSY)

45

Neymar uses his fame and money to **help other people**. In **2014**, he created an **education and sports facility** to help the people who live near his **old neighbourhood**.

THANKS, NEYMAR!

Neymar Jr Institute, *Praia Grande*

CHAPTER 5

SANTOS STAR

Santos FC is one of the most famous clubs in Brazil. **Football legend Pelé** played for Santos in the **1960s**.

Neymar signed for the **Santos youth team in 2003.** He could hardly believe it – this was **a dream come true!**

He was even earning money for playing football, which was a huge help to his family. And he was only **12 years old!**

As a **small, skinny teenager,** it could be tough playing at Santos. **Bigger, older players** didn't like being tricked by Neymar's **clever skills . . .**

DINK!

OWWWW!

. . . so they would *FOUL* him!

50

Neymar trained **VERY, very hard.** His coach, Lima, turned him into a **playmaker.** He started to create and **score lots and lots of goals!**

When he was **13,** Neymar had a trial at **Real Madrid.** Star players like **Zinedine Zidane,** (Brazilian) **Ronaldo** and **David Beckham** were in the squad at the time.

WOW!

Zidane

Ronaldo

Beckham

Madrid wanted to sign him, but Neymar and
his dad said,

Neymar made **his first-team debut** as a substitute for **Santos** against Oeste on **7 March 2009.**

The fans were already calling him *THE NEW PELÉ.*

Against **Mogi Mirim** a few days later,
Neymar started the game – **and scored.**
He was on his way.

Neymar's **stunning performances** were getting him noticed all over the world. In **2010,** Premier League club **West Ham United** offered Santos **£12 MILLION** for Neymar.

Once again, he said, **"No, thanks."**

And when **Chelsea** offered even more, Neymar still decided to **stay with Santos.**

Avram Grant
(West Ham coach)

Carlo Ancelotti
(Chelsea coach)

Neymar's first of **TWO GOALS** in this match was an **absolutely stunning** solo effort. A long dribble, a left-footed flick around the defender and finishing with a **right-foot smash!**

This goal **won** the **Puskas Award** for the season's **most beautiful goal.**

NEYMAR'S SANTOS HONOURS

CAMPEONATO PAULISTA WINNER

2010

2011

2012

COPA DO BRASIL WINNER

2010

WORLD SOCCER YOUNG PLAYER OF THE YEAR

2011

COPA LIBERTADORES

2011

Neymar is Santos' all-time **top scorer.**

NEYMAR'S SANTOS STATS
2009-2013

APPEARANCES	GOALS	ASSISTS
225	136	65

SOUTH AMERICAN
FOOTBALLER OF
THE YEAR
2011
2012

CHAPTER 6

BARCELONA BOUND

In 2013, Neymar was one of the **hottest prospects in world football.** Lots of big clubs tried to sign him, including

REAL MADRID

CHELSEA

MANCHESTER UNITED

In the end, he signed for **Barcelona** for

an estimated

£49 MILLION!

Neymar was introduced to more than **56,000**

fans at the Barcelona stadium, the **Nou Camp!**

He would play alongside this guy!

SEASON DEBUTS

Neymar made his **La Liga debut** for **Barcelona** against **Levante** on **18 August 2013**.

Three days later he scored his first **goal** for the club - a header in the **Supercopa de España** against **Atlético Madrid**.

FUMP!

26 OCTOBER 2013

LA LIGA

BARCELONA 2-1 REAL MADRID

This was Neymar's first **El Clasico.**
Barcelona faced a **Real Madrid** team
that included **Cristiano Ronaldo** and
Gareth Bale.

Neymar picked up a pass from
Andrés Iniesta and - *BOOM*
- scored in the **19th minute.**

BOOM!

Then he set up **Alexis Sánchez** for Barcelona's second goal.

THE **BARCELONA FANS** HAD A **NEW HERO!**

Lionel Messi

11 DECEMBER 2013

CHAMPIONS LEAGUE GROUP STAGE

BARCELONA 6-1 CELTIC

Neymar's goal just before half-time was his **first ever goal** in the **Champions League**.

His **second** was an **absolutely fantastic** left-footed shot.

And his **58th-minute goal** brought Neymar his first Barcelona **hat-trick.**

AWESOME!

On **15 February 2014,** at home to **Rayo Vallecano,** Neymar picked up the ball on the halfway line, dribbled down the middle of the pitch and - **BAM!** - scored with an awesome right-footed shot.

NEYMAR'S 2013-2014 RECORD

APPEARANCES	GOALS	ASSISTS
41	15	15

Only **Lionel Messi** scored more Champions League goals for **Barcelona** in **2013-14**.

CHAPTER 7

TREBLE MAGIC

LA LIGA HIGHLIGHTS 2014-2015

THE BEST BITS OF A SPECIAL SEASON IN LA LIGA FOR NEYMAR AND BARCELONA.

13 SEPTEMBER 2014

BARCELONA 2-0 ATHLETIC BILBAO

Neymar, assisted by **Lionel Messi,** scored his **first** and **second goals** of the season to see off Bilbao in style.

27 SEPTEMBER 2014

BARCELONA 6-0 GRANADA

Starting with **THREE of the SIX** goals to complete his **first La Liga hat-trick,** Neymar enjoyed a run of **SIX** goals in **FOUR** La Liga matches.

11 JANUARY 2015

BARCELONA 3-1 ATLÉTICO MADRID

This was the first game in which **Neymar, Lionel Messi** and new signing **Luis Suárez** each scored a goal.

Neymar

Messi

Suárez

Barcelona **secured the La Liga** title by beating **Atlético Madrid** on **17 May 2015**.

POSITION	TEAM	POINTS
1	**BARCELONA**	**94**
2	**REAL MADRID**	92
3	**ATLÉTICO MADRID**	78

It was the **23rd time** Barcelona had won La Liga.

BOP!

WHEEEEE!

Neymar scored **22 goals** and recorded **9 assists.** He was Barcelona's **second-highest scorer** in La Liga behind **Lionel Messi** (with 43 goals).

TROPHY #1

COPA KINGS

In the **Copa del Rey,** Neymar scored **TWO goals** against **Elche** in the **last 16 . . .**

. . . TWO goals against **Atlético Madrid** in the **quarter-finals . . .**

. . . and TWO goals in the **semi-finals** against **Villareal.**

In the **final,** Neymar scored the second
of Barcelona's **three goals** as they beat
Athletic Bilbao 3-1.

It was Barcelona's 27th **Copa del Rey** win.

With **SEVEN goals**, Neymar was
joint top-scorer in the competition.

TROPHY #2

#1

In the **2014–15 Champions League,** Barcelona played **Paris Saint–Germain FOUR** times. Neymar scored in each match - including **TWO GOALS** in the **second leg** of the quarter-final.

12 MAY 2015

CHAMPIONS LEAGUE SEMI-FINAL 2ND LEG

BAYERN MUNICH 3-2 BARCELONA

(3-5 AGGREGATE)

Neymar had scored the **last goal** in the **first leg** and **TWO GOALS** in the first 30 minutes of the second leg. **Bayern** fought back in the **second half** to make it 3-2, but Barcelona were in the final.

Barcelona had qualified for the **Champions League** final for the **eighth time**.

FINAL FANTASTIC

6 JUNE 2015

CHAMPIONS LEAGUE FINAL

JUVENTUS 1-3 BARCELONA

Juventus had also won their **league and cup** at home - the winner of this match would be **TREBLE** champions!

THWACK!

Barcelona took an early lead, but Juventus equalised in the second half. **Luis Suárez** put them ahead again and then **Neymar** **scored a late goal to win 3–1!**

Barcelona were **Champions of Europe** and **TREBLE** winners!

TROPHY #3

#1

#2

RECORD SEASON

2014-15 was an incredible, **record-breaking season** for Neymar and Barcelona.

Barcelona became the first team to win a treble for **the second time.**

They last did it in **2008-09.**

ON THE DOUBLE

ON THE DOUBLE

In the **2015–16 season,** Neymar scored **24 goals** in La Liga, including **FOUR** in one game against Rayo Vallecano.

Barcelona and Neymar won La Liga for the **second season in a row!**

Neymar scored a late goal in the **Copa del Rey final** as **Sevilla** were beaten **2–0.**

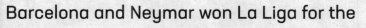

Another season and an incredible **DOUBLE** win. Neymar was piling up medals year on year.

MAGIC MSN

2014–15 was the first season that Lionel **Messi,** Luis **Suárez** and **Neymar** played together. They were known as **MSN.**

Together, **MSN** netted an incredible **122 goals** in the **treble-winning season,** and then an even more awesome **131 goals** in the **2015–2016 season.**

In 2015, **MSN** scored more goals than the **whole Real Madrid team.**

2016-17 HIGHLIGHTS

BIG MOMENTS IN NEYMAR'S FINAL SEASON AT THE NOU CAMP.

8 MARCH 2017

CHAMPIONS LEAGUE ROUND OF 16, 2ND LEG

BARCELONA 6-1 PARIS SAINT-GERMAIN

Neymar was a **nightmare for PSG** once again. He **scored TWICE** and **assisted two more goals** to soundly beat the Paris side.

2 APRIL 2017

LA LIGA

GRANADA 1-4 BARCELONA

*Neymar scored his **100th GOAL** for Barcelona in injury time.*

14 MAY 2017

LA LIGA

LAS PALMAS 1-4 BARCELONA

*Neymar scored his **third** Barcelona **HAT-TRICK** in this away match at the end of the season.*

Neymar and Barcelona won the **Copa del Rey** for the third season in a row.

NEYMAR AT BARCELONA

SEASON	APPEARANCES	GOALS	ASSISTS
2013–14	41	15	15
2014–15	51	39	10
2015–16	49	31	25
2016–17	45	20	26
TOTAL	186	105	76

"I LIKE NEYMAR A LOT. HE IS A BIT LIKE ME."

Cristiano Ronaldo

CHAPTER 8

BRAZIL STAR

While Neymar was **at Santos,** lots of Brazilian fans and players wanted to see their **18–year–old** star play for **Brazil** at the **2010 World Cup.**

But the coach said, "NO."

NEYMAR'S NOT READY. HE WILL HAVE TO WAIT. **SORRY.**

Dunga, Brazil's coach in 2010

In the end, Neymar made his debut in a **friendly against the USA,** just after the World Cup.

And of course — he scored!

MEDAL MAGIC

Neymar scored **THREE** goals at the **2012 Olympics in London.** He won a **silver medal** when Brazil lost the final 2-1 to **Mexico.**

The **2016 Olympics** were in **BRAZIL,** in the city of **Rio de Janeiro.** Neymar was the captain in his homeland – **what an honour!**

Neymar scored after **14 seconds** in the 2016 semi-final – the fastest goal in Olympic history.

In the final against Germany, the match went to a **penalty shoot-out.** And guess who scored the winner?

In **2013,** Brazil hosted the **Confederations Cup.** Neymar scored **FOUR goals** in the tournament, including one in the final as Brazil beat **Spain 3–0.**

Neymar won the **Golden Ball** as the Player of the Tournament.

Neymar has scored **four hat-tricks** for

Brazil, including one in a friendly against

Japan in **2014,** where he scored all

FOUR GOALS as Brazil won **4–0.**

WORLD CUP WOE

In **2014**, the **eyes of the world** were on **Neymar**, when the **World Cup** was held in **Brazil**.

Neymar scored **TWO GOALS** in the opening game against **Croatia**.

BOOM!

But then . . . Neymar was injured in the **quarter-final with Colombia.** He missed the **rest of the tournament.**

Without Neymar, Brazil lost the semi-final **7–1** to **Germany.** Football fans around the world were **stunned.**

SPORTS NEWS

BRAZIL OUT OF WORLD CUP!

7-1

It was Brazil's **worst ever** defeat at a **World Cup.**

BRAZIL'S GREATEST?

Only Pelé has scored more goals for Brazil than Neymar. Can he break the record?

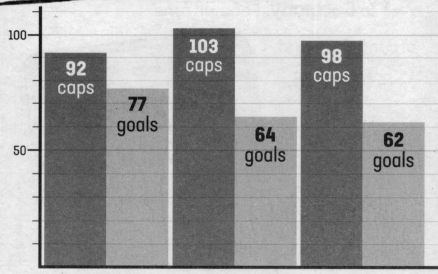

92 caps
77 goals

103 caps
64 goals

98 caps
62 goals

100

50

PELÉ
1957-1971

NEYMAR
2010-

RONALDO
1994-2011

HOW DOES NEYMAR COMPARE WITH SOME OF THE OTHER GREAT BRAZILIAN PLAYERS?

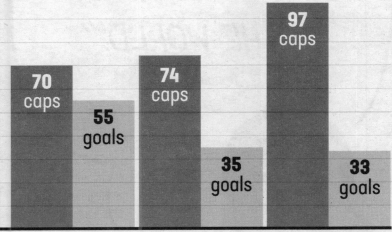

70
caps

55
goals

74
caps

35
goals

97
caps

33
goals

ROMÁRIO
1987-2005

RIVALDO
1993-2003

RONALDINHO
1999-2013

CHAPTER 9

PARIS CALLING

In **2017,** the French club **Paris Saint-Germain** had a plan to win lots of trophies. So they signed **Neymar from Barcelona.**

For an estimated . . .

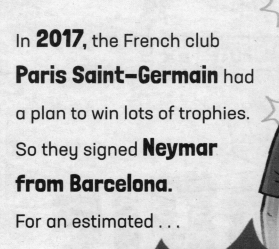

£200 MILLION!

Neymar was **THE MOST EXPENSIVE FOOTBALLER IN THE HISTORY OF THE WORLD.**

That's enough to buy a **private jet,** a fleet of **sports cars** and a **luxury yacht . . .**

TREBLE TRIO

Neymar, with team-mates **Kylian Mbappé** and **Edinson Cavani,** were known together as *MCN.*

Mbappé

Cavani

In 2017-18 the **three forwards** scored **87 GOALS** between them.

And PSG won the
Coupe de la Ligue . . .

The **Coupe de France** . . .

The **Coupe de France** . . .

And **LIGUE 1** . . .

Neymar was a

TREBLE WINNER

in his first season.

FANTASTIC!

109

PSG HIGHLIGHTS

17 JANUARY 2018

LIGUE 1

PSG 8-0 DIJON

Neymar was on **FIRE** in this match, scoring **FOUR** of PSG's **EIGHT** goals.

He scored with a free kick . . .

A shot with his left foot . . .

An awesome solo effort . . .

And a penalty!

3 OCTOBER 2018

CHAMPIONS LEAGUE GROUP STAGE

PSG 6-1 RED STAR BELGRADE

Another PSG **goal-fest,** with Neymar scoring his first **Champions League hat-trick** for PSG.

BOFF!

NEYMAR'S PSG STATS AND RECORDS

SEASON	APPEARANCES	GOALS	ASSISTS
2017–18	30	28	16
2018–19	28	23	13
2019–20	27	19	12
TOTAL	85	70	41

Knock, knock.

Who's there?

Willy.

Willy who?

Willy score again?

LIGUE 1 PLAYER
OF THE YEAR
2017-18

LIGUE 1 PLAYER
OF THE MONTH
DECEMBER 2017
JANUARY 2020

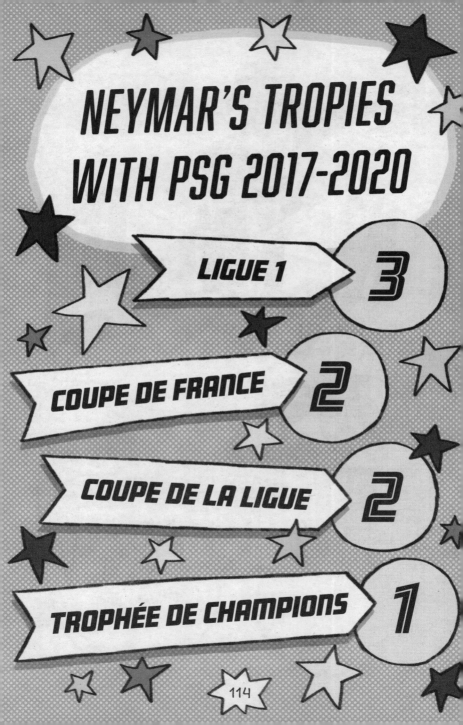

CELEBRATION TIME

When he scores one of his many **fantastic goals,** Neymar is always ready with a **crazy celebration!**

BEING BRAZILIAN, HE LOVES A BIT OF DANCING!

Neymar has missed lots of games at PSG because of **injury and suspensions**. But when he does play he scores **lots of goals** and is **AWESOME** at setting up more for his team-mates.

Neymar is a **speedy player** and **full of tricks.** He even falls over with amazing style!

During the 2018 World Cup, the social media hashtag **#neymarchallenge** showed videos of lots of people falling over like Neymar . . .

AAAAA
AAAAAA
AAAAAA
AAAAAA
AAAAAA
AAAAAA
AAAAAA
AARGH!

Despite his **falling over** and **occasional playacting,** Neymar is still one of the most **entertaining** and awesome strikers in the game.

TROPHIES AND AWARDS

SOME OF THE **BRILLIANT WINS** NEYMAR HAS NOTCHED UP SO FAR:

CAMPEONATO PAULISTA
2010
2011
2012

RECOPA SUDAMERICANA
2012

COPA LIBERTADORES
2011

LA LIGA
2014-15
2015-16

CONFEDERATIONS CUP
2013

COPA DEL REY
2014-15
2015-16
2016-17

QUIZ TIME!

How much do you know about **NEYMAR?** Try this quiz to find out, then test your friends!

1. What is the special version of football that Neymar played as a boy?

---

2. Who was Neymar's first football coach?

---

3. In which year did Neymar sign for the Santos youth team?

---

4. Name one of the two English Premier League clubs that tried to sign Neymar from Santos.

---

5. How many goals did Neymar score for Santos?

---

6. In which season did Neymar win the treble with Barcelona?

---

7. Which players were M and S in MSN?

---

8. In which year did Neymar win an Olympic Gold medal?

---

9. What was the estimated fee that PSG paid for Neymar?

---

10. How many goals did Neymar score for PSG in 2017-18?

The answers are on the next page *but no peeking!*

ANSWERS

1. Futsal
2. Betinho
3. 2003
4. West Ham or Chelsea
5. 136

6. 2014-15
7. Lionel Messi and Luis Suárez
8. 2016
9. £200 million
10. 28

NEYMAR:
WORDS YOU NEED TO KNOW

Campeonato Paulista
The top regional football league in São Paulo, Brazil.

Coupe de France
France's main knockout cup competition

Coupe de la Ligue
The second knockout football competition in France. "The French League Cup"

La Liga
The top football league in Spain.

Ligue 1
The top football league in France.

Trophée des Champions
Trophy awarded to the winner of a match between the Ligue 1 champions and the Coupe de France winners.

UEFA Champions League
European club competition held every year. The winner is the best team in Europe.

ABOUT THE AUTHORS

Simon's first job was at the Science Museum, making paper aeroplanes and blowing bubbles big enough for your dad to stand in. Since then he's written all sorts of books about the stuff he likes, from dinosaurs and rockets, to llamas, loud music and of course, football. Simon has supported Ipswich Town since they won the FA Cup in 1978 (it's true – look it up) and once sat next to Rio Ferdinand on a train. He lives in Kent with his wife and daughter, two tortoises and a cat.

Dan has drawn silly pictures since he could hold a crayon. Then he grew up and started making books about stuff like trucks, space, people's jobs, *Doctor Who* and *Star Wars*. Dan remembers Ipswich Town winning the FA Cup but he

didn't watch it because he was too busy making a Viking ship out of brown paper. As a result, he knows more about Vikings than football. Dan lives in Suffolk with his wife, son, daughter and a dog that takes him for very long walks.